DECISIONS

Finding

God's
Will

J. I.
PACKER

WITH DALE & SANDY LARSEN

**6 studies
for individuals or groups**

CHRISTIAN BASICS BIBLE STUDIES

With Guidelines for
Leaders & Study Notes
NIV Text Included

ivp

InterVarsity Press
Downers Grove, Illinois, USA
Leicester, England

InterVarsity Press
P.O. Box 1400, Downers Grove, IL 60515, USA
38 De Montfort Street, Leicester LE1 7GP, England

©1996 by J. I. Packer

*InterVarsity Press® is the book-publishing division of InterVarsity Christian Fellowship®, a student
movement active on campus at hundreds of universities, colleges and schools of nursing in the
United States of America, and a member movement of the International Fellowship of Evangelical
Students. For information about local and regional activities, write Public Relations Dept.,
InterVarsity Christian Fellowship, 6400 Schroeder Rd., P.O. Box 7895, Madison, WI 53707-7895.*

This study guide is based on and adapts material from Finding God's Will *©1985 by J. I. Packer,
originally published as chapter twenty of* Knowing God, *©1975 by J. I. Packer and used with
permission of Hodder & Stoughton Limited, London.*

*Inter-Varsity Press, England, is the book-publishing division of the Universities and Colleges
Christian Fellowship (formerly the Inter-Varsity Fellowship), a student movement linking
Christian Unions in universities and colleges throughout the United Kingdom and the Republic of
Ireland, and a member movement of the International Fellowship of Evangelical Students. For
information about local and national activities write to UCCF, 38 De Montfort Street, Leicester
LE1 7GP.*

Cover photograph: Michael Goss

Cover background: Cowgirl Stock Photography ©1991

USA ISBN 0-8308-2014-0
UK ISBN 0-85111-376-1

Printed in the United States of America ⊗

21   20   19   18   17   16   15   14   13   12   11   10   9   8   7   6   5   4

13   12   11   10   09   08   07   06   05   04   03   02   01   00

Getting the Most Out of Christian Basics Bible Studies

Knowing Christ is where faith begins. From there we grow through the essentials of discipleship: Bible study, prayer, worship, Christian community and much more. We learn to set godly priorities, overcome spiritual opposition and witness to others. These are the topics woven into each of the Christian Basics Bible Studies. Working through this series will help you become a more mature Christian.

What Kind of Guide Is This?
The studies are not designed to merely tell you what one person thinks. Instead, through inductive study, they will help you discover for yourself what Scripture is saying. Each study deals with a particular passage—rather than jumping around the Bible—so that you can really delve into the author's meaning in that context.

The studies ask three different kinds of questions. *Observation* questions help you to understand the content of the passage by asking about the basic facts: who, what, when, where and how. *Interpretation* questions delve into the meaning of the passage. *Application* questions help you discover its implications for growing in Christ. These three keys unlock the treasures of the biblical writings and help you live them out.

This is a thought-provoking guide. Each question assumes a variety of answers. Many questions do not have "right" answers, particularly questions that aim at meaning or application. Instead, the questions should inspire users to explore the passage more thoroughly.

This study guide is flexible. You can use it for individual study, but it is also great for a variety of groups—student, professional, neighborhood or church groups. Each study takes about forty-five minutes in a group setting or thirty minutes in personal study.

How They're Put Together
Each study is composed of four sections: opening paragraphs and questions to help you get into the topic, the NIV text and questions that invite study of the passage, questions to help you apply what you have learned, and a suggestion for prayer.

The workbook format provides space for writing a response to each question. This format is ideal for personal study and allows group members to prepare in advance for the discussion and/or write down notes during the study. This space can form a permanent record of your thoughts and spiritual progress.

At the back of the guide are study notes which may be useful for leaders or for individuals. These notes do not give "the answers," but they do provide additional background information on certain questions to help you through the difficult spots. The

"Guidelines for Leaders" section describes how to lead a group discussion, gives helpful tips on group dynamics and suggests ways to deal with problems which may arise during the discussion. With such helps, someone with little or no experience can lead an effective group study.

Suggestions for Individual Study

1. If you have not read the book or booklet suggested in the "further reading" section, you may want to read the portion suggested before you begin your study.

2. Read the introduction. Consider the opening questions and note your responses.

3. Pray, asking God to speak to you from his Word about this particular topic.

4. Read the passage reproduced for you in the New International Version. You may wish to mark phrases that seem important. Note in the margin any questions that come to your mind as you read.

5. Use the questions from the study guide to more thoroughly examine the passage. Note your findings in the space provided. After you have made your own notes, read the corresponding study notes in the back of the book for further insights.

6. Reread the entire passage, making further notes about its general principles and about the way you intend to use them.

7. Move to the "commit" section. Spend time prayerfully considering what the passage has to say specifically to your life.

8. Read the suggestion for prayer. Speak to God about insights you have gained. Tell him of any desires you have for specific growth. Ask him to help you as you attempt to live out the principles described in that passage.

Suggestions for Members of a Group Study

Joining a Bible study group can be a great avenue to spiritual growth. Here are a few guidelines that will help you as you participate in the studies in this guide.

1. These studies focus on a particular passage of Scripture— in depth. Only rarely should you refer to other portions of the Bible, and then only at the request of the leader. Of course, the Bible is internally consistent. Other good forms of study draw on that consistency, but inductive Bible study sticks with a single passage and works on it in depth.

2. These are discussion studies. Questions in this guide aim at helping a group discuss together a passage of Scripture in order to understand its content, meaning and implications. Most people are either natural talkers or natural listeners. Yet this type of study works best if people participate more or less evenly. Try to curb any natural tendency to either excessive talking or excessive quiet. You and the rest of the group will benefit.

3. Most questions in this guide allow for a variety of answers. If you disagree with someone else's comment, gently say so. Then explain your own point of view from the passage before you.

4. Be willing to lead a discussion, if asked. Much of the preparation for leading has already been accomplished in the writing of this guide.

5. Respect the privacy of people in your group. Many people speak of things within the context of a Bible study/prayer group that they do not want to be public knowledge. Assume that personal information spoken within the group setting is private, unless you are specifically told otherwise. And don't talk about it elsewhere.

6. We recommend that all groups follow a few basic guidelines and that these guidelines be read at the first session. The guidelines, which you may wish to adapt to your situation, are the following:

a. Anything said in this group is considered confidential and will not be discussed outside the group unless specific permission is given to do so.

b. We will provide time for each person present to talk if he or she feels comfortable doing so.

c. We will talk about ourselves and our own situations, avoiding conversation about other people.

d. We will listen attentively to each other.

e. We will pray for each other.

7. Enjoy your study. Prepare to grow. God bless.

Suggestions for Group Leaders

There are specific suggestions to help you in leading in the guidelines for leaders and in the study notes at the back of this guide. Read the guidelines for leaders carefully, even if you are only leading one group meeting. Then you can go to the section on the particular session you will lead.

Introduction: Wondering What to Do?

We face many difficult questions in life: How should we spend our time and our resources? What work should we be involved in? Where should we live? and so on. Sometimes we wonder what God would say if we could just sit down and ask him what to do.

God has given us the resources to make decisions—Scripture, the Holy Spirit, prayer, Christian community and the ability to reason. By using these resources to make decisions we grow into the people he intends us to be.

Once I received a letter from a minister who felt obliged to leave his congregation and denomination. Like Abraham, he went out uncertain of his destination. In his letter, he quoted a hymn by Charles Wesley on the sovereignty and security of God's guidance:

Captain of Israel's host and Guide

Of all who seek the land above,

Beneath Thy shadow we abide,

The cloud of Thy protecting love;

Our strength, Thy grace; our rule, Thy Word;

Our end, the glory of the Lord.

Guidance, like all God's acts of blessing under the covenant of grace, is a sovereign act. Not merely does God will to guide us in the sense of showing us his way, that we may walk in it. He wills also to guide us in the more fundamental sense of ensuring that whatever happens, whatever mistakes we may make, we shall come home safely. We will slip and stray, but the everlasting arms are beneath us. We shall be caught, rescued, restored. This is God's promise; this is how good he is. The right context for discussing guidance is one of confidence in the God who will not let us ruin our souls. Our concern, therefore, should be more for his glory than for our security—for that is already taken care of. With this assurance we then step out in confidence to discover God's will for us.

For further reading: This guide builds on ideas found in the booklet Finding God's Will. *After each study there is a reference to the related portion of that booklet. J. I. Packer also wrote on guidance in* Hot Tub Religion *(pp. 105-37), available from Tyndale House Publishers.*

Study One
God Will Guide You

Psalm 25

Do you trust that God will guide you through life? Not all Christians do.

Today, knowledge of God has been obscured—turned, in effect, into ignorance of God—by the twisting of our thoughts about him. The reality of God's rule, God's speech, God's independence, God's moral goodness, even God's personality has been questioned not only outside the church but also inside it. This has made it hard for many to believe that divine guidance can exist at all. How can it if God is not the sort of being who can, or will, give it? That is what, in one way or another, all these doubts imply.

God does have a plan for us, and Scripture promises that divine guidance will help us know God's plan. This is the topic of Psalm 25.

Open —————————————————————————

☐ Recall a time you're sure the Lord guided you in a decision. How did God's guidance come to you?

What has been the outcome (so far)?

☐ How do you typically go about asking God for guidance?

__ I pray in times of crisis.

__ I look for confirming signs.

__ I try to act on general principles from Scripture.

__ I don't proceed until I feel an inner certainty.

__ I pray about everything.

__ I seek counsel from godly people.

__ I am unsure about how to receive guidance from God.

__ Other: _____

☐ In what ways are you dissatisfied with how you make decisions?

Study

Read Psalm 25:

¹To you, O LORD, I lift up my soul; ²in you I trust, O my God. Do not let me be put to shame, nor let my enemies triumph over me. ³No one whose hope is in you will ever be put to shame, but they will be put to shame who are treacherous without excuse.

[4]Show me your ways, O LORD, teach me your paths; [5]guide me in your truth and teach me, for you are God my Savior, and my hope is in you all day long. [6]Remember, O LORD, your great mercy and love, for they are from of old. [7]Remember not the sins of my youth and my rebellious ways; according to your love remember me, for you are good, O LORD. [8]Good and upright is the LORD; therefore he instructs sinners in his ways. [9]He guides the humble in what is right and teaches them his way. [10]All the ways of the LORD are loving and faithful for those who keep the demands of his covenant. [11]For the sake of your name, O LORD, forgive my iniquity, though it is great. [12]Who, then, is the man that fears the LORD? He will instruct him in the way chosen for him. [13]He will spend his days in prosperity, and his descendants will inherit the land. [14]The LORD confides in those who fear him; he makes his covenant known to them. [15]My eyes are ever on the LORD, for only he will release my feet from the snare. [16]Turn to me and be gracious to me, for I am lonely and afflicted. [17]The troubles of my heart have multiplied; free me from my anguish. [18]Look upon my affliction and my distress and take away all my sins. [19]See how my enemies have increased and how fiercely they hate me! [20]Guard my life and rescue me; let me not be put to shame, for I take refuge in you. [21]May integrity and uprightness protect me, because my hope is in you. [22]Redeem Israel, O God, from all their troubles!

1. What indications do you see that David, the psalm writer, fully expected the Lord to guide him?

2. How would you describe David's stance before the Lord?

3. In order for people to receive the Lord's guidance, what conditions did David consider necessary (vv. 9-14)?

4. How did David acknowledge his own failings (vv. 7, 11, 18)?

5. Besides his own inward sin, David faced external opposition and problems (vv. 2-3, 16-20). Nevertheless, he expected to know God's guidance through it all. What qualities of the Lord are implied in David's assurance?

6. Besides guidance, what else did David ask for in his prayer?

7. How does David's attitude toward God's guidance compare or contrast with your own, both over the years and now?

Commit

☐ In what decisions do you feel the most need for God's guidance?

☐ In what decisions do you doubt or wonder whether God can or will guide you?

Honestly express to the Lord your confidence—or your doubts—in his guidance. As much as you can, commit to him a decision you have to make soon.

For further reading: pages 3-7 of Finding God's Will.

Study Two
The Spirit's Leading

Acts 15:22-35

*I*n her "fanaticism papers" Hannah Whitall Smith tells of a woman who, each morning, having consecrated the day to the Lord as soon as she woke, "would then ask Him whether she was to get up or not," and would not stir till "the voice" told her to dress.

As she put on each article she asked the Lord whether she was to put it on, and very often the Lord would tell her to put on the right shoe and leave off the other; sometimes she was to put on both stockings and no shoes; and sometimes both shoes and no stockings; it was the same with all the articles of dress.[1]

This pathetic story is typical of what can happen when we look uncritically to the Holy Spirit for guidance in all things. When should we look to the Spirit for guidance? This passage in Acts provides some clues.

Open

☐ What experiences of the Holy Spirit's guidance have you had?

☐ Why does waiting for the voice of the Holy Spirit sometimes result in behavior such as that described in the introduction?

☐ By contrast, how do you think Christians ought to rely on the Holy Spirit for guidance?

Study

Read Acts 15:22-35:

[22] Then the apostles and elders, with the whole church, decided to choose some of their own men and send them to Antioch with Paul and Barnabas. They chose Judas (called Barsabbas) and Silas, two men who were leaders among the brothers. [23] With them they sent the following letter:

The apostles and elders, your brothers,

To the Gentile believers in Antioch, Syria and Cilicia:

Greetings.

²⁴We have heard that some went out from us without our authorization and disturbed you, troubling your minds by what they said. ²⁵So we all agreed to choose some men and send them to you with our dear friends Barnabas and Paul— ²⁶men who have risked their lives for the name of our Lord Jesus Christ. ²⁷Therefore we are sending Judas and Silas to confirm by word of mouth what we are writing. ²⁸It seemed good to the Holy Spirit and to us not to burden you with anything beyond the following requirements: ²⁹You are to abstain from food sacrificed to idols, from blood, from the meat of strangled animals and from sexual immorality. You will do well to avoid these things. Farewell.

³⁰The men were sent off and went down to Antioch, where they gathered the church together and delivered the letter. ³¹The people read it and were glad for its encouraging message. ³²Judas and Silas, who themselves were prophets, said much to encourage and strengthen the brothers. ³³After spending some time there, they were sent off by the brothers with the blessing of peace to return to those who had sent them. ³⁵But Paul and Barnabas remained in Antioch, where they and many others taught and preached the word of the Lord.

---

1. What words and phrases in this Scripture refer to choices and decisions made by these early Christians?

2. How would you paraphrase the phrase in verse 28, "it seemed good to the Holy Spirit and to us"?

_____

3. In order to use that phrase, what attitudes needed to be present in the hearts of the apostles and elders?

_____

4. Which of your attitudes might need to change in order for your heart to be primed to sense what is good to the Holy Spirit?

_____

5. What evidence do you look for to know whether a particular course of action "seems good to the Holy Spirit"?

_____

6. How were the events in verses 30-35 a confirmation of Paul and Barnabas's decision?

7. One Christian was distressed when the members of his church board disagreed about taking a stand on a controversial issue. He protested, "If the Holy Spirit is guiding all of them, they'll all be led the same direction and will agree completely." How would you respond to that statement?

Commit

☐ While we long to discover what the Holy Spirit is saying to us about a particular problem, we may be ignoring what the Spirit has already said. Consider some areas of your life in which you might be resisting or drowning out the Holy Spirit's voice. How will you listen more earnestly to the Spirit?

Decide in advance to obey the Holy Spirit's promptings during the coming week.

Pray for sensitivity to the Spirit of God as he speaks in Scripture, in your conscience, in circumstances and in the voices of other people.
   For further reading: pages 9-17 of Finding God's Will.

---

[1]Published posthumously by Ray Strachey, first as *Religious Fanaticism* (1928), then as *Group Movements of the Past and Experiments in Guidance* (1934).

Study Three
Making Big Decisions
Colossians 1:1-14

S hould I contemplate marriage or not? Should I marry this person or not? Should we plan to have another child? Should I join this church or that one? Which profession should I follow?

When we hear the word *guidance*, we think of specific problems. These are the questions that shape our lives and affect our joy or sorrow. But what does Scripture have to say in answer to these questions? No biblical text told me to propose to the lady who is now my wife, or seek ordination, or start my ministry in England or buy my large old car.

The basic form of divine guidance is the presentation to us of positive ideals as guidelines for all our living. "Be the kind of person Jesus was." This is how God guides us through the Bible.

Open

☐ What major decision is facing you for which there seems to be no definite right or wrong answer?

☐ How might your decision affect your relationship with Jesus Christ?

☐ How might your decision affect your Christian witness?

Study

Read Colossians 1:1-14:

¹Paul, an apostle of Christ Jesus by the will of God, and Timothy our brother,

²To the holy and faithful brothers in Christ at Colosse:

Grace and peace to you from God our Father.

³We always thank God, the Father of our Lord Jesus Christ, when we pray for you, ⁴because we have heard of your faith in Christ Jesus and of the love you have for all the saints — ⁵the faith

and love that spring from the hope that is stored up for you in heaven and that you have already heard about in the word of truth, the gospel ⁶that has come to you. All over the world this gospel is bearing fruit and growing, just as it has been doing among you since the day you heard it and understood God's grace in all its truth. ⁷You learned it from Epaphras, our dear fellow servant, who is a faithful minister of Christ on our behalf, ⁸and who also told us of your love in the Spirit.

⁹For this reason, since the day we heard about you, we have not stopped praying for you and asking God to fill you with the knowledge of his will through all spiritual wisdom and understanding. ¹⁰And we pray this in order that you may live a life worthy of the Lord and may please him in every way: bearing fruit in every good work, growing in the knowledge of God, ¹¹being strengthened with all power according to his glorious might so that you may have great endurance and patience, and joyfully ¹²giving thanks to the Father, who has qualified you to share in the inheritance of the saints in the kingdom of light. ¹³For he has rescued us from the dominion of darkness and brought us into the kingdom of the Son he loves, ¹⁴in whom we have redemption, the forgiveness of sins.

1. What attitude toward the Lord runs throughout this passage?

2. Paul gave thanks for the Colossians' faith in Jesus and love for

one another (v. 3). What was the source of their faith and love?

3. What did Paul ask God to do for the Colossian Christians (vv. 9-14)?

4. We all make vocational choices for which we do not find specific answers in Scripture—regarding work, where to live, how to spend time and money, and so on. Consider the things Paul prayed for in verses 9-12. How would each one help you make such vocational decisions?

5. How do the promises of what God has already provided for us go beyond any of our immediate needs for guidance?

6. What encouragement do you find in this Scripture that God is vitally concerned with your vocational choices?

Commit

☐ What Scriptural principles have a bearing on your most pressing vocational choices?

☐ Consider whether you might be waiting for a "word from the Lord" when he has already given you sufficient Scriptural principles to guide you. How can you go ahead on what you already know?

Pray the prayer of Colossians 1:9-12 for yourself. Include giving thanks to the Lord as verse 12 says.

For further reading: pages 7-9, 11-12, 16-17 of Finding God's Will.

Study Four
Advice: With a Little Help from Our Friends

Exodus 18:13-26

*E*ven with right ideas about guidance in general, however, it is still easy to go wrong with difficult choices. No area of life bears clearer witness to the frailty of human nature. One way to check our own inclinations is to listen to the advice of others.

Scripture is emphatic on the need for us to take advice. "The way of a fool seems right to him, but a wise man listens to advice" (Proverbs 12:15). It is a sign of conceit and immaturity to ignore advice in major decisions. There are always people who know the Bible, human nature, and our own gifts and limitations better than we do. Even if we cannot finally accept their advice, good will come to us from carefully weighing what they say.

Even those who give advice to others need to receive counsel.

In this passage we see how Jethro's advice helps Moses out of a difficult and potentially overwhelming situation.

Open

☐ When it comes to asking for advice,

__ I gather all the opinions I can.

__ I trust nobody but myself.

__ I've gotten burned too many times by following bad advice.

__ I have certain people whose advice I rely on.

__ too much advice just confuses things.

__ other: _____

_____

☐ When have you been helped by someone's wise advice?

☐ How do you decide who to ask for advice?

Study

Read Exodus 18:13-26:

¹³The next day Moses took his seat to serve as judge for the people, and they stood around him from morning till evening. ¹⁴When his father-in-law saw all that Moses was doing for the people, he said, "What is this you are doing for the people? Why do you alone sit as judge, while all these people stand around you from morning till evening?"

[15]Moses answered him, "Because the people come to me to seek God's will. [16]Whenever they have a dispute, it is brought to me, and I decide between the parties and inform them of God's decrees and laws."

[17]Moses' father-in-law replied, "What you are doing is not good. [18]You and these people who come to you will only wear yourselves out. The work is too heavy for you; you cannot handle it alone. [19]Listen now to me and I will give you some advice, and may God be with you. You must be the people's representative before God and bring their disputes to him. [20]Teach them the decrees and laws, and show them the way to live and the duties they are to perform. [21]But select capable men from all the people—men who fear God, trustworthy men who hate dishonest gain—and appoint them as officials over thousands, hundreds, fifties and tens. [22]Have them serve as judges for the people at all times, but have them bring every difficult case to you; the simple cases they can decide themselves. That will make your load lighter, because they will share it with you. [23]If you do this and God so commands, you will be able to stand the strain, and all these people will go home satisfied."

[24]Moses listened to his father-in-law and did everything he said. [25]He chose capable men from all Israel and made them leaders of the people, officials over thousands, hundreds, fifties and tens. [26]They served as judges for the people at all times. The difficult cases they brought to Moses, but the simple ones they decided themselves.

---

1. What problem did Moses fail to recognize?

2. Why do you think Moses hadn't discerned his difficulty?

3. What was good about the advice of Moses' father-in-law?

4. What various ways could Moses have reacted to his father-in-law's advice?

5. What do Moses' actions in verses 24-26 reveal about his character?

6. How do you normally react to advice from your relatives?

7. How do you react to advice in general?

8. What attitudes do you need to cultivate in order to be more receptive to good advice?

Commit

☐ Consider who you might ask to advise you on a decision you need to make. What characteristics are you looking for in a potential advisor?

☐ In what areas do you need to be more open to the opinions of others?

Knowing that advisors must be carefully chosen, ask the Lord for wisdom about who to ask for advice about various decisions.

For further reading: page 19 of Finding God's Will.

Study Five
Suspect Yourself

Jonah 1

God's word was clear to Jonah: "Go to the great city of Nineveh and preach against it." Jonah went in the opposite direction—Tarshish.

We can recognize rationalizations in others that we completely overlook in ourselves. Like Jonah, it is easy for us to persuade ourselves that the direction we receive from God is not to do that unappealing thing, but to do the thing we want to do. In particular, feelings that have an ego-boosting, escapist, self-indulging or self-aggrandizing base must be detected and discredited, not mistaken for guidance.

We need to ask ourselves why we "feel" a particular course to be right and make ourselves give reasons. We also need to keep praying: "Search me, O God, and know my heart; test me and know my anxious thoughts. See if there is any offensive way in me, and lead me in the way everlasting" (Psalm 139:23-24). Jonah's story is a reminder of how our personal biases can influence our openness to God.

Open

☐ I distrust my own motives when I have to make decisions about:

__ my job   __ my closest relationships

__ social activities   __ church activities

__ doing things that will put   __ spending money
me in the spotlight

__ I don't normally dis-   other:_____
trust my motives.

☐ I wish I *had* distrusted my own motives when I decided . . .

☐ I'm glad that I reconsidered my motives and changed my mind about . . .

Study

Read Jonah 1:

¹ The word of the LORD came to Jonah son of Amittai: ²"Go to the great city of Nineveh and preach against it, because its wickedness has come up before me."

³But Jonah ran away from the LORD and headed for Tarshish. He went down to Joppa, where he found a ship bound for that port. After paying the fare, he went aboard and sailed for Tarshish to flee from the LORD.

⁴Then the LORD sent a great wind on the sea, and such a violent storm arose that the ship threatened to break up. ⁵All the sailors were afraid and each cried out to his own god. And they threw the cargo into the sea to lighten the ship.

But Jonah had gone below deck, where he lay down and fell into a deep sleep. ⁶The captain went to him and said, "How can you sleep? Get up and call on your god! Maybe he will take notice of us, and we will not perish."

⁷Then the sailors said to each other, "Come, let us cast lots to find out who is responsible for this calamity." They cast lots and the lot fell on Jonah.

⁸So they asked him, "Tell us, who is responsible for making all this trouble for us? What do you do? Where do you come from? What is your country? From what people are you?"

⁹He answered, "I am a Hebrew and I worship the LORD, the God of heaven, who made the sea and the land."

¹⁰This terrified them and they asked, "What have you done?" (They knew he was running away from the LORD, because he had already told them so.)

¹¹The sea was getting rougher and rougher. So they asked him, "What should we do to you to make the sea calm down for us?"

¹²"Pick me up and throw me into the sea," he replied, "and it will become calm. I know that it is my fault that this great storm has come upon you."

¹³Instead, the men did their best to row back to land. But they could not, for the sea grew even wilder than before. ¹⁴Then they cried to the LORD, "O LORD, please do not let us die for taking this man's life. Do not hold us accountable for killing an innocent man, for you, O LORD, have done as you pleased." ¹⁵Then they took Jonah and threw him overboard, and the raging sea grew

calm. [16]At this the men greatly feared the LORD, and they offered
a sacrifice to the LORD and made vows to him.

[17]But the LORD provided a great fish to swallow Jonah, and
Jonah was inside the fish three days and three nights.

---

1. What did God call Jonah to do?

What would have been difficult about obeying?

---

2. While we sometimes have difficulty discerning God's will, there
was nothing vague about his command to Jonah. How did Jonah
respond?

---

3. In your opinion, what are some reasons Jonah may have felt
compelled to run away from God?

4. What are some circumstances in which you have felt like running away from God or from what God wanted you to do?

5. How did Jonah's decision affect the lives of other people (vv. 4-5, 14-16)?

6. After Jonah was exposed as the cause of the storm, what did he reveal to the sailors about his recognition of his actions and their consequences (vv. 7-12)?

7. How have others been hurt by your avoidance of God's will?

8. After Jonah admitted his fault (v. 12), how did the Lord mercifully provide for his rescue (v. 17)?

Commit

☐ In what parts of your life are you avoiding what God has already asked you to do?

☐ What form does your ship to Tarshish take?

☐ Perhaps the Lord has sent or is sending a storm to turn you back, or perhaps he is letting you go your way for now, just as he let the ship sail for a while before sending the violent wind. What will you do about God's persistent call to obey?

Pray about any areas where you are fleeing from God's guidance. Turn back to the Lord and once again commit yourself to obeying him. Even if doing his will is costly, trust him to take care of you.
  For further reading: pages 19-22 of Finding God's Will.

Study Six
Smooth Sailing Ahead?

Exodus 13:20—14:14

*O*ne of the great mysteries of faith is that making the right choice does not necessarily lead to a trouble-free course thereafter. Sometimes following God leads to a new crop of problems that otherwise would not have arisen—isolation, criticism, abandonment by friends, practical frustrations of all sorts. Does this mean the choice was wrong?

Possibly—and we should take the opportunity to check the original guidance carefully. But trouble is not necessarily a sign of being off-track. The experience of the Israelites' crossing the Red Sea is an example of that fact.

Open

☐ Which of the following statements do you agree with?

__ If I follow the Lord's guidance, things will work better than if I hadn't followed God.

__ Life is never easy, even if you follow the Lord.

__ Sometimes life gets tougher
   after I've done what I thought
   was right.

__ What counts is to obey,
   not what happens after-
   ward.

__other:_____

☐ The previous study showed us how Jonah's life got tough when he ran from the Lord. Even when we obey God, life is sometimes hard. Consider a time you encountered new difficulties because you decided to obey God. What made you expect—or not expect—that this would happen?

How did you deal with the new troubles?

Study

Moses was sent by God to convince Pharaoh to release his thousands of Hebrew slaves and let them leave Egypt. Pharaoh took a lot of convincing, but plagues from God finally persuaded him. The Israelites made a fast escape on the night of the first Passover. Once his slaves were gone, Pharaoh had second thoughts and came after them.

Read Exodus 13:20—14:14:

[20]After leaving Succoth they camped at Etham on the edge of the desert. [21]By day the LORD went ahead of them in a pillar of cloud to guide them on their way and by night in a pillar of fire to

give them light, so that they could travel by day or night. [22] Neither the pillar of cloud by day nor the pillar of fire by night left its place in front of the people.

[1] Then the LORD said to Moses, [2] "Tell the Israelites to turn back and encamp near Pi Hahiroth, between Migdol and the sea. They are to encamp by the sea, directly opposite Baal Zephon. [3] Pharaoh will think, 'The Israelites are wandering around the land in confusion, hemmed in by the desert.' [4] And I will harden Pharaoh's heart, and he will pursue them. But I will gain glory for myself through Pharaoh and all his army, and the Egyptians will know that I am the LORD." So the Israelites did this.

[5] When the king of Egypt was told that the people had fled, Pharaoh and his officials changed their minds about them and said, "What have we done? We have let the Israelites go and have lost their services!" [6] So he had his chariot made ready and took his army with him. [7] He took six hundred of the best chariots, along with all the other chariots of Egypt, with officers over all of them. [8] The LORD hardened the heart of Pharaoh king of Egypt, so that he pursued the Israelites, who were marching out boldly. [9] The Egyptians—all Pharaoh's horses and chariots, horsemen and troops—pursued the Israelites and overtook them as they camped by the sea near Pi Hahiroth, opposite Baal Zephon.

[10] As Pharaoh approached, the Israelites looked up, and there were the Egyptians, marching after them. They were terrified and cried out to the LORD. [11] They said to Moses, "Was it because there were no graves in Egypt that you brought us to the desert to die? What have you done to us by bringing us out of Egypt? [12] Didn't we say to you in Egypt, 'Leave us alone; let us serve the Egyptians'? It would have been better for us to serve the Egyptians than to die in the desert!"

[13]Moses answered the people, "Do not be afraid. Stand firm and you will see the deliverance the LORD will bring you today. The Egyptians you see today you will never see again. [14]The LORD will fight for you; you need only to be still."

---

1. How did God consistently make his guidance clear to the Israelites (13:21-22)?

---

2. How did God put Israel in a situation which would specifically cause Pharaoh to pursue them (14:1-4)?

---

3. From 14:4, what insight do you get about the Lord's purposes in trouble?

---

4. When the Egyptian army appeared, what did the Israelites conclude (14:10-12)?

5. In what circumstances have you concluded that it would have been better to stay as you were than to follow God in obedience (as Israel said in 14:12)?

6. What did the Lord (through Moses) promise the frightened Israelites (14:13-14)?

7. How have you seen God's promise come true in your own life? (Think especially of times when obeying God at first only made things "worse.")

Commit

☐ In what areas of your life do you struggle with longing to "return to Egypt" and go back to when things seemed easier?

☐ How can you apply God's promises to your own areas of fear or regret right now?

☐ How will you "be still" and let the Lord fight for you (v. 14)?

Confess to the Lord any ways that you resent or regret your decision to follow him. Commit your past, present and future to his care. Above all, determine to keep following his guidance no matter what.

For further reading: pages 22-24 of Finding God's Will.

Guidelines for Leaders

Leading a Bible discussion can be an enjoyable and rewarding experience. But it can also be intimidating—especially if you've never done it before. If this is how you feel, you're in good company.

Remember when God asked Moses to lead the Israelites out of Egypt? Moses replied, "O Lord, please send someone else to do it" (Exodus 4:13). But God gave Moses the help (human and divine) he needed to be a strong leader.

Leading a Bible discussion is not difficult if you follow certain guidelines. You don't need to be an expert on the Bible or a trained teacher. The suggestions listed below can help you to effectively fulfill your role as leader—and enjoy doing it.

Preparing for the Study
1. As you study the passage ahead of time, ask God to help you understand it and apply it in your own life. Unless this happens, you will not be prepared to lead others. Pray too for the various members

of the group. Ask God to open your hearts to the message of his Word and motivate you to action.

2. Read the introduction to the entire guide to get an overview of the subject at hand and the issues which will be explored.

3. Be ready for the "Open" questions with a personal story or example. The group will be only as vulnerable and open as its leader.

4. As you begin preparing for each study, read and reread the assigned Bible passage to familiarize yourself with it. You may want to look up the passage in a Bible so that you can see its context.

5. This study guide is based on the New International Version of the Bible. That is what is reproduced in your guide. It will help you and the group if you use this translation as the basis for your study and discussion.

6. Carefully work through each question in the study. Spend time in meditation and reflection as you consider how to respond.

7. Write your thoughts and responses in the space provided in the study guide. This will help you to express your understanding of the passage clearly.

8. It might help you to have a Bible dictionary handy. Use it to look up any unfamiliar words, names or places. (For additional help on how to study a passage, see chapter five of *Leading Bible Discussions*, IVP.)

9. Take the final (application) questions and the "Commit" portion of each study seriously. Consider what this means for your life, what changes you may need to make in your lifestyle and/or what actions you can take in your church or with people you know. Remember that the group will follow your lead in responding to the studies.

Leading the Study

1. Be sure everyone in your group has a study guide and Bible. Encourage the group to prepare beforehand for each discussion by reading the introduction to the guide and by working through the questions in the study.

2. At the beginning of your first time together, explain that these studies are meant to be discussions, not lectures. Encourage the members of the group to participate. However, do not put pressure on those who may be hesitant to speak during the first few sessions.

3. Begin the study on time. Open with prayer, asking God to help the group understand and apply the passage.

4. Have a group member read the introductory paragraph at the beginning of the discussion. This will remind the group of the topic of the study.

5. Every study begins with a section called *Open*. These "approach" questions are meant to be asked before the passage is read. They are important for several reasons.

First, there is always a stiffness that needs to be overcome before people will begin to talk openly. A good question will break the ice.

Second, most people will have lots of different things going on in their minds (dinner, an exam, an important meeting coming up, how to get the car fixed) that have nothing to do with the study. A creative question will get their attention and draw them into the discussion.

Third, approach questions can reveal where our thoughts or feelings need to be transformed by Scripture. That is why it is especially important not to read the passage before the approach question is asked. The passage will tend to color the honest reactions people would otherwise give, because they feel they are supposed to think the way the Bible does.

6. Have a group member read aloud the passage to be studied.

7. As you ask the questions, keep in mind that they are designed to be used just as they are written. You may simply read them aloud. Or you may prefer to express them in your own words.

There may be times when it is appropriate to deviate from the study guide. For example, a question may already have been answered. If so, move on to the next question. Or someone may raise an important question not covered in the guide. Take time to discuss it, but try to keep the group from going off on tangents.

8. Avoid answering your own questions. Repeat or rephrase them if necessary until they are clearly understood. An eager group quickly becomes passive and silent if members think the leader will give all the *right* answers.

9. Don't be afraid of silence. People may need time to think about the question before formulating their answers.

10. Don't be content with just one answer. Ask, "What do the rest of you think?" or, "Anything else?" until several people have given answers to a question.

11. Acknowledge all contributions. Be affirming whenever possible. Never reject an answer. If it is clearly off-base, ask, "Which verse led you to that conclusion?" or, "What do the rest of you think?"

12. Don't expect every answer to be addressed to you, even though this will probably happen at first. As group members become more at ease, they will begin to truly interact with each other. This is one sign of healthy discussion.

13. Don't be afraid of controversy. It can be stimulating! If you don't resolve an issue completely, don't be frustrated. Move on and keep it in mind for later. A subsequent study may solve the problem.

14. Periodically summarize what the group has said about the passage. This helps to draw together the various ideas mentioned and gives continuity to the study. But don't preach.

15. Don't skip over the application questions at the end of each study. It's important that we each apply the message of the passage to ourselves in a specific way. Be willing to get things started by describing how you have been affected by the study.

Depending on the makeup of your group and the length of time you've been together, you may or may not want to discuss the "Commit" section. If not, allow the group to read it and reflect on it silently. Encourage members to make specific commitments and to write them in their study guide. Ask them the following week how they did with their commitments.

16. Conclude your time together with conversational prayer. Ask for God's help in following through on the commitments you've made.

17. End on time.

Many more suggestions and helps are found in *The Big Book on Small Groups, Small Group Leaders' Handbook* and *Good Things Come in Small Groups* (IVP). Reading through one of these books would be worth your time.

Study Notes

Study One. God Will Guide You. Psalm 25.

Purpose: To reassure ourselves that the Lord is willing and able to give us guidance for all kinds of decisions.

Question 1. Notice the confidence in the prayer in verses 4-5 and the statements in verses 12-14. While these are cries from the writer's heart, there is no wishful thinking.

Question 2. David showed confidence but neither arrogance nor flippancy. The Lord's guidance was something he assumed, yet not something he took for granted or thought he had earned.

Question 3. Twice David mentions God's covenant—first that God shows his ways to those who keep his covenant (v. 10) and then that God makes his covenant known to those who fear him (v. 14). The covenant David knew was the old covenant of the Law. Christians are under the new covenant of Christ. In both cases God's promise of guidance proves true, and in both cases it is conditional on our obedience to what we know of God's will. Paul argued that though we are free from the Law, we are not free to disobey God and live in sin (Romans 6).

Questions 4-5. Despite the conditions of humility and obedience mentioned in question 3, David knew himself to be a sinner (see vv. 7, 18). While we need to repent and get back on the path to obedience as soon as we recognize sin in our lives, we don't need to fear that failure cuts off God's guidance forever. We can take comfort in the promise of verse 8: The Lord "instructs *sinners* in his ways." Our God is a God who not merely restores but also takes up our mistakes and follies into his plan for us and brings good out of them. This is part of the wonder of his gracious sovereignty.

Study Two. The Spirit's Leading. Acts 15:22-35.
Purpose: To see and apply an example of the Holy Spirit's leading in the life of the church.
Question 1. The first Christians were almost all Jews. It was not until years after the life of Jesus that the church became open to Gentiles accepting the Jewish Messiah. The occasion of this letter was a conflict over how rigidly the new Gentile converts ought to keep the Jewish law, particularly whether males had to be circumcised. After Peter, Barnabas and Paul gave convincing accounts of God's work in the hearts of Gentiles, James recommended a stance of mercy and freedom (see Acts 15:1-21). The church was confident that their policy was the result of the Holy Spirit's leading as well as their own rational discussion.
Question 3. They had to believe that the Holy Spirit could and would guide them into what was best. They also needed to be committed to following God's will once they knew it. That meant deciding in advance to cooperate with the Holy Spirit; otherwise what seemed good to the Spirit would not have seemed so good to the church!
Question 4. First would be any preconceived ideas of the direction the Holy Spirit is going to lead you. Another stumbling block is conditional acceptance of the Spirit's leading—being willing to follow

only if he leads you a certain way.

Question 5. In his book about decision-making, Garry Friesen makes this interesting comment on Acts 15:28:

The Holy Spirit was included as a coauthor of the decision. Does that mean that the conclusions of the council were supernaturally dictated by God? He certainly did give special guidance on other occasions in Acts. But in this case, in the absence of any direct statement to that effect, a better explanation would be that the Holy Spirit had *already given* His guidance before the council ever met [through examples of the Gentiles accepting Christ without submitting to circumcision]. . . . For these reasons, the church leaders could write that their decision "seemed good" to the Holy Spirit as well as to them. (*Decision Making and the Will of God*, with J. Robin Maxson [Portland, Ore.: Multnomah, 1980], p. 186.)

Question 7. Disagreements over nonessential issues were common in the early church and have continued to be common through the centuries. Romans 14 says that because of different background and conscience, believers may sincerely differ over secondary matters. In fact the church is not even in agreement about which items are secondary! Then there is the reality that for a church board to always agree on every detail of the Holy Spirit's guidance, every member would have to be hearing and following the Spirit absolutely perfectly at all times—ideal, but not the norm.

Study Three. Making Big Decisions. Colossians 1:1-14.
Purpose: To rely on the principles of Scripture in our vocational decision-making.

Question 4. Clearly the knowledge of God's will is necessary for making vocational decisions as well as any other decisions. The importance of the other qualities may be less obvious. A life lived worthy of the Lord is vital, simply because a person who is *not* living such a life needs to get down to business with God about issues of character before seeking convenient signposts about job or marriage. The knowledge *of God* goes beyond the knowledge of his particular will for a decision; it is the close relationship in which we know his love and want to please him. Power, endurance and patience will help us meet the demands of obeying God's guidance where it is difficult. Thankfulness lifts our obedience out of drudgery into the joy of pleasing God.

Question 5. The fundamental guidance that God gives to shape our lives—the instilling, that is, of the basic convictions, attitudes, ideals and value judgments by which we are to live—is not a matter of inward promptings apart from the Word. It is the pressure on our consciences of the portrayal in the Word of God's character and will, which the Spirit enlightens us to understand and apply for ourselves. Only within the limits of *this* guidance does God prompt us inwardly in matters of vocational decision.

Question 6. The God portrayed here is vitally involved with his children. Especially in verses 9-14 we see that he does not want to keep us in the dark. He wants us to know him and be close to him; he wants our lives to please him, and he wants us to do right. This is a God who will not leave us drifting in the details of our lives.

Study Four. Advice: With a Little Help from Our Friends. Exodus 18:13-26.

Purpose: To be open to hearing the advice of others and to weigh it wisely.

Question 1. Moses had led the enslaved Israelites out of their captivity in Egypt. Now they were on their long journey to the land

God had promised them. As we would expect among a large group of people traveling together under stressful circumstances, disputes came up. Moses acted as judge for all those disputes. His father-in-law, Jethro, "the priest of Midian," visited him and was impressed with all God had done, but warned Moses that he was wearing himself and the people out by judging all of their cases himself (Exodus 18:1-12).

Question 2. Because of his God-given leading role in freeing the Israelites, Moses may have assumed that all the work of leadership was still up to him. Many of us assume we are indispensable and need to stay in control of the situation.

Question 7. Elisabeth Elliot writes:

It is a good thing to talk over a decision with a friend. The times when we find ourselves entirely alone in the making of a decision are rare. Nearly always there are others who will be affected by what we decide, and usually some of these can be consulted. A person who loves God and has had some experience in finding his will is the kind we should look for. . . . It may be that you cannot find anyone who can advise you, but you can find someone who will pray with you. . . . There is a special power in the union and communion of two or more agreed on asking for a single specific thing. (*A Slow and Certain Light* [Waco, Tex.: Word, 1973], pp. 108-9.)

Study Five. Suspect Yourself. Jonah 1.
Purpose: To become realistic about how easily we mistake our own desires for God's will, and to make ourselves give reasons when we feel a certain course is right.

Question 3. The Bible doesn't tell us all the reasons Jonah fled, but history tells us that Nineveh was the capital of the Assyrians, who were cruel and ruthless oppressors. The beginning of chapter 4 indicates that Jonah suspected that God would forgive the repentant Ninevites and not bring judgment on them—which is exactly what happened.

Question 5. Jonah's disobedience did not happen in a vacuum. It brought a violent storm which threatened to smash the ship, terrified everyone aboard and caused the loss of the cargo. Later, however, Jonah's repentance made believers out of the pagan sailors.

Question 6. Jonah was not in the dark about what was going on. He knew he had deliberately tried to avoid the Lord, and he was discovering that it can't be done. We should give Jonah credit for his honesty at this point. He was willing to take some consequences for his actions, though perhaps he was not ready to go to Nineveh yet.

Question 7. When we flee from the Lord, we are thinking only of protecting ourselves from inconvenience, confrontation, being unmasked or some other cost of obedience. Like Jonah, we don't think about others who will get caught in the storm we cause. The disobedience of one person has consequences for many. Examples range from breaking a promise to pick up a friend, leaving her freezing on a street corner, to bombing a building and killing hundreds.

Study Six. Smooth Sailing Ahead? Exodus 13:20—14:14.
Purpose: To prepare ourselves for difficulties which may result from obeying God, and to commit ourselves to continuing to obey no matter what.

Questions 1-2. Trouble should always be treated as a call to consider one's ways. But trouble is not necessarily a sign of being off-track, for as the Bible declares in general that "many are the afflictions of the righteous" (Psalm 34:19 NRSV), so it teaches in particular that following God's guidance regularly leads to upsets and distresses that we would otherwise have escaped. Jonah (study 5) was running away when God sent the storm. The Israelites were perfectly in the path of obedience, following God's cloud and fire, when Pharaoh's army came after them. We might say, "What's the difference? Both were equally unpleasant!" But the cause and significance of the two are distinct, and perhaps only the person going through the circumstance really knows the difference.

Questions 3 and 6. Scripture tells us the outcome of Pharaoh's pursuit: God did gain glory for himself by delivering Israel (Exodus 14:15-31). In present circumstances we don't have that hindsight; we can only trust God to bring us through safely.

Questions 4-5. The Israelites' conclusion was based on panic in the face of immediate danger. Yet the danger was real, not imagined. They really were in trouble because they had followed God. For proof of the truth that following God's guidance brings trouble, look at the life of the Lord Jesus himself. No human life has ever been so completely guided by God, and no human being has ever qualified so comprehensively for the description "a man of sorrows."

Question 7. After Israel's miraculous deliverance at the Red Sea, they went on with their journey only to start complaining and doubting God again. Through the following centuries, the Scriptures kept reminding Israel of this pivotal event in their history, when obeying God brought them both trouble and deliverance. Our memories are short; we need to keep reminding ourselves that trouble is not the end of the story.

Christian Basics Bible Studies from InterVarsity Press

Christian Basics are the keys to becoming a mature disciple. The studies in these guides, based on material from some well-loved books (which can be read along with the studies), will take you through key Scripture passages and help you to apply biblical truths to your life. Each guide has six studies for individuals or groups.

Certainty: Know Why You Believe by Paul Little with Scott Hotaling. Faith means facing hard questions. Is Jesus the only way to God? Why does God allow suffering and evil? These questions need solid answers. These studies will guide you to Scripture to find a reasonable response to the toughest challenges you face.

Character: Who You Are When No One's Looking by Bill Hybels with Dale and Sandy Larsen. Courage. Discipline. Vision. Endurance. Compassion. Self-sacrifice. The qualities covered in this Bible study guide provide a foundation for character. With this foundation and God's guidance, we can maintain character even when we face temptations and troubles.

Christ: Basic Christianity by John Stott with Scott Hotaling. God himself is seeking us through his Son, Jesus Christ. But who is this Jesus? These studies explore the person and character of the man who has altered the face of history. Discover him for the first time or in a new and deeper way.

Christ's Body: The Community of the King by Howard Snyder with Robbie and Breck Castleman. What is God's vision for the church? What is my role? What are my spiritual gifts? This guide helps illumine God's plan for the church and for each of us as a part of it.

Commitment: My Heart—Christ's Home by Robert Boyd Munger with Dale and Sandy Larsen. What would it be like to have Christ come into the home of our hearts? Moving from the living room to the study to the recreation room with him, we discover what he desires for us. These studies will take you through six rooms of your heart. You will be stretched and enriched by your personal meetings with Christ in each study.

Decisions: Finding God's Will by J. I. Packer with Dale and Sandy Larsen. Facing a big decision? From job changes to marriage to buying a house, this guide will give you the biblical grounding you need to discover what God has in store for you.

Excellence: Run with the Horses by Eugene Peterson with Scott Hotaling. Life is difficult. Daily we must choose whether to live cautiously or courageously. God calls us to live at our best, to pursue righteousness, to sustain a drive toward excellence. These studies on Jeremiah's pursuit of excellence with God's help will motivate and inspire you.

Lordship: Basic Discipleship by Floyd McClung with Dale and Sandy Larsen. Have you ever felt like a spiritual failure? Does the Christian life seem like a set of rules that are impossible to follow? This guide contains the biblical keys to true discipleship. By following them you'll be liberated to serve God in every aspect of your life.

Perseverance: A Long Obedience in the Same Direction by Eugene Peterson with Dale and Sandy Larsen. When the going gets tough, what does a Christian do? This world is no friend to grace. God has given us some resources, however. As we grow in character qualities like hope, patience, repentance and joy, we will grow in our ability to persevere. The biblical passages in these studies offer encouragement to continue in the path Christ has set forth for us.

Prayer: Too Busy Not to Pray by Bill Hybels with Dale and Sandy Larsen. There's so much going on—work, church, school, family, relationships: the list is never-ending. Someone always seems to need something from us. But time for God, time to pray, seems impossible to find. These studies are designed to help you slow down and listen to God so that you can respond to him.

Priorities: Tyranny of the Urgent by Charles Hummel. Have you ever wished for a thirty-hour day? Every week we leave a trail of unfinished tasks. Unanswered letters, unvisited friends and unread books haunt our waking moments. We desperately need relief. This guide is designed to help you put your life back in order by discovering what is *really* important. Find out what God's priorities are for you.

Scripture: God's Word for Contemporary Christians by John Stott with Scott Hotaling. What is the place of Scripture in our lives? We know it is important—God's Word to us—but how can it make a difference to us each day? In this guide John Stott will show you the power Scripture can have in your life. These studies will help you make the Bible your anchor to God in the face of the temptation and corruption that are all around.

Spiritual Warfare: The Fight by John White with Dale and Sandy Larsen. As a Christian, you are a sworn foe of the legions of hell. They will oppose you as you obey Christ. Life with Jesus can be an exhilarating and reassuring experience of triumph over evil forces. But the battle never ends. This guide will help you prepare for war.

Witnessing: How to Give Away Your Faith by Paul Little with Dale and Sandy Larsen. If you want to talk about Jesus, but you're not sure what to say—or how to say it—this Bible study guide is for you. It will deepen your understanding of the essentials of faith and strengthen your confidence as you talk with others.

Work: Serving God by What We Do by Ben Patterson with Dietrich Gruen. "I can serve God in church, but can I serve him on the job?" In the factory, in the office, in the home, on the road, on the farm—Ben Patterson says we can give glory to God wherever he calls us. Work, even what seems to us the most mundane, is what God created us for. He is our employer. These studies will show you how your work can become meaningful and satisfying.

Worship: Serving God with Our Praise by Ben Patterson with Dietrich Gruen. Our deepest need can be filled only as we come to our Creator in worship. This is the divine drama in which we are all invited to participate, not as observers but as performers. True worship will transform every part of our lives, and these studies will help you to understand and experience the glory of praising God.